First Time

BY ANTHONY HOWELL

Poetry

Inside the Castle
Imruil
Oslo
Notions of a Mirror
Why I May Never See the Walls of China
Howell's Law

Novel

In the Company of Others

ANTHONY HOWELL
first time in japan

Anvil Press Poetry

Published in 1995
by Anvil Press Poetry Ltd
69 King George Street London SE10 8PX

Copyright © Anthony Howell 1995

This book is published
with financial assistance from
The Arts Council of England

Designed and composed by Anvil
Photoset in Plantin by Typestream
Printed and bound in England
by The Arc & Throstle Press, Todmorden, Lancs
Distributed by Password, Manchester

ISBN 0 85646 263 2

A catalogue record for this book
is available from the British Library

ACKNOWLEDGEMENTS

'Highly Inflammable Horizons', 'First Time in Japan' and 'Melancholy Isle' came out in *Is* magazine. 'The Watering Hole' and 'The Larder Scene' appeared in *The Yellow Crane*. 'A Household God' appeared in *The Poetry Review*. 'A Young Mother' came out in *The Critical Quarterly* and was also anthologized in *The Exact Change Yearbook*. 'Splices' appeared in *Ambit*. 'The Erotic Windmill' was first published as a *Turret* poem-card. 'The Ballad of the Sands' appeared in *The Swansea Review*.

The reproduction on the cover of this book is of 'First Time in Japan' by Eric Fischl.

CONTENTS

1 *The Old Roman*

Highly Inflammable Horizons	9
First Time in Japan	10
Talking of Michelangelo	11
Melancholy Isle	12
Intercity	14
The Watering Hole	15
The Immigrant	16
The Listener	18
Seeking after Pleasure	20
A Household God	21
Splices	24
A Young Mother	26
Bizarre Bazaars	27
An Interview with the Sinn Fein	28
The Erotic Windmill	29
Oasis	30
Between Functions	31
The Larder Scene	32
Castel Gandolfo	34
Death Lane	36

2 *The Ballad of the Sands*   41

NOTES   61

1

The Old Roman

HIGHLY INFLAMMABLE HORIZONS

CJ tinkers with his outboard
While I goggle up.
His keel rocks in mid-lagoon.
I flip down to coral brains,
The neon luminations of the reef.
I spot the stoplight, the spotted trunkfish,
Then I meet the shark.
He mooches *his* way
Around corrupted antlers.

My yellow flippers
Would put anyone off
– Morays, barracudas.
I blow out my snorkel
And bring it up with CJ.
He insists they're friendly.
My bus takes me home
Past humped or Friesian cattle
Every other palm:

'No smoking, no nuts in shell,
No snow-cones please.
And please remove all sharp edge weapon
From the rear pockets.'

FIRST TIME IN JAPAN

You are here by the power of your imagination,
Businessman, acquaintance of my father,
Being transferred through space, not time,
On the wings of Pan-Am, to a family bath
We all take quite naturally without clothes on.
You're denied your glasses in our bath-house,
Which is why you squint at me,
Crumpled yet unfolded, contradictory.
Were you a quarter-back, once upon a time?
Your big hands could still provide a tractor seat,
Man from the mid-west, who squints at me.
But you're the naked subject, not Susannah:
It's the elders who should not be seen.
Their sagging flesh spells money and withdraws
Into that androgyny achieved
After much protocol and obedience to the system.
Your scrutiny's too hard for my own good,
Though not for yours. Voluptuous on the edge,
You feel delicious, vulnerable,
Having doffed some armadillo suit.
Actually I'm studying the famous
Terracottas from the town of Kerch:
Among them there are senile pregnant hags
Who laugh at us – for nothing is completed,
Even age combines with some new life,
Since an old man's nipples can be sensitive.

TALKING OF MICHELANGELO

The women occupy the lower
Third of the upholstered lift
Or lift cream with teaspoons
Among tree-pots, their glasses
Raised like visors onto foreheads.

They talk intelligently about
What they see, set their elbows
On the table-top and swivel rings
Round lean fingers; palms propping chins
As they almost claw their perches.

Their hands love their own hands,
Whose fingertips form chapels
Or lower the glasses needed to read
The menu: parrot-throated,
They peer at each other askance.

Noble and self-confident, they never
Undress; blown larger than life,
Inanimate and spread a little thin
Across the showing space, but still
With anxieties worth millions.

I think of a helpless
Girl on a bed, unable to
Protect her utterly looked-at
Labia; hopeless, battered by
Life more, seen at the *Marlborough*.

MELANCHOLY ISLE

Twice a week they beach their rippling hill.
Rhythmic hands will rope it in, to heap
Slithering gills on silver caked with sand.
The catch gasps. Ebony and ivory
Jostle near its shudders, leaping back
When stainless barracuda whip the ankles
Everyone comes away with at least a couple
Of wrasse for the pot, but suddenly
A gale will carry debris down the gullies.
Mops toss. Nasty little apples
Whirling in dissolved clay, as the spates collide,
Go spinning on, into turgid rollers.
Petals stain. The beach is largely mud
Littered with splintered bamboo, tubers.
Only birds on stilts make fastidious moves
As tourists pick and choose in the boutique.

Now the sun again inserts its needles
Under the skin, sliding through the optics
Of a palm to irritate the haughty-looking Indian.
That ugly sea could never be her element:
She peels off her No-Mans-Land teeshirt
To dive into the hibiscus-shaped pool.
If this were Eden, and if she were Eve,
She'd trade my orchid for a manchineel.
Wild orchid seedlings are caught stars clinging
By day to the telephone strings above lanes
Decked with the Christmas chains of vines.
School signs, with British caps and satchels,

Rusted silhouettes of Master Hugo
And his sister, say, seem out of place
On Sundays, when frocks are being shown off,
And big men in wellingtons sharpen their machetes.

INTERCITY

Cables lope along by streamlined carriages,
And orderly canals have shadows
Uniform with bridges. But you look out
At the backsides of places, hinderparts
To mansions, patched together lean-tos.
Practical indecencies: underpants on tyre-stacks,
Paths to disgraces only a few people use:
The dens of clutch specialists, muffler fitters,
Barely reachable tracts of the unspeakable.
This is the unconscious side of the animal
Betrayed by things it would like to forget:
Small, scruffy woods, suitable for rape,
Deadly-looking pools, the slapdash of terraces
Which speed and distance try to sentimentalize:
Cuttings hacked through the body, dead
Lorry acreages overrun by brambles . . .

THE WATERING HOLE

There's a big crowd in the Beverley tonight:
Lads that sharp they look lemony
Are wearing out the crushed flower carpet.
Dappled partings and suffused crew-cuts
Here occult obsolete methods of transport.
Silhouettes removed from frosted glass
Delineate spiked fruit, flames and so forth.
The boy-scouts are about to bump the statue:
Short sleeves make biceps look the bigger,
While bike-boys look lissom in their leathers:
Boot-soles stropped against the rail.
Sheer legs are tucked beneath a chair.
Nice boys look tougher cropped of hair,
Broad girls look lovelier in their tresses.
Those with uncomfortable noses are made
Acutely aware by the knowing shake of the head
With the half-smile – 'I'm sorry, darl –.'
They make messes of the big ashtrays:
Long white filters wear their kisses.
Many of the men sport patches on their hearts
And appreciate ten-denier stay-puts,
Fuchsia blouses, camisoles and hair.
Every Sunday morning the conscientious girls
Colourize their samplers under streams of urine.
The bike-boys keep to one end of the bar,
The boy-scouts to the other – not real
Bike-boys, not genuine boy-scouts either.

THE IMMIGRANT

My eucalypt has just about
Grown tall enough
To screen the battered wives
Going in and out
Of the toilet round the back
Directly opposite.

The species never hides
As much as Europeans might
Being designed to let the breeze
And light pass easily through it,
So as not to die of heat
In its native climate.

Scarcely thicker
Than my wrist as yet,
Its lissom trunk is supported
By polythene bags
Knotted tight
To a headless broomstick.

Local birds of the smaller sort
Sporadically perch in it,
Given the weather allows.
Now it leans towards the wall,
While its constant leaves
Toss in the worsening gale.

Grown a few more feet,
Back in the antipodes,
Such a tree would shed its bark.
Here it hasn't risked
This customary stripping off,
But no tree ever looked more naked.

THE LISTENER

You put the kettle on
And stroll into the living-room
To slide in the disk:
Then you go outside
To throw stale slices
At little birds,
Hoping that the cats
Will be nice to them.

Lemon yellow leaves
Are swept by a hand
Which is like a breeze.
Still in your dressing-gown
You climb up the stairs
To some quite spindly
Particulars of theme
As the harpist plucks

And picks her way between
The oboes and robust
Bowing from the strings.
Entering your study
With your mug of tea,
You notice little birds
Flitting from the cherry
To the locust tree.

Listen, you could swear
That they've begun.
Yes, you're pretty sure,
Despite the concerto
Which is everywhere.
When they begin
Their conversation
Tends to wear thin.

A few lovely sighs
Increase in intensity.
But didn't you select
This concerto
So that they'd forget
About the noise?
They're only making love
In your head, you know.

Meanwhile the harp
Unwinds its song:
Allegro moderato
Sprinkles an arpeggio
So distinct you long
To catch the drips
And touch each string
With your fingertips.

SEEKING AFTER PLEASURE

Dilys wants us to get a washing machine.
There's no need to suck in the tum.
Nobody can see it very clearly.

Not that I can take this for long.
Just beyond that clouded door
There's an oasis of ordinary air.

Blinded, I step out again
Into some chilly shower,
Rub myself, then sip Ribena.

Men sit passive, seem to come to rest,
Lulled by the jacuzzi's less furious
Droolings; its cycle expired.

Please shower first, it says.
Having done so, I grip the hand-rail
To let myself down into its trough.

Say I risk a nasty rash?
Never mind. I'm quite prepared
To catch something from this lovely girl

Sharing with me, resting freckled arms:
Up to her neck in mutual foam,
She looks towards a fern

As faucets churn us into cream.
She could give me herpes or eczema.
I am an ambitious man.

A HOUSEHOLD GOD

Polar white, I am their private Christmas.
My regular defrosting requires no assistance.
Melted ice falls into my trough, drains away
And evaporates. Pulling at the finger-pull
Moulded into my trim lights up a glittering display.
Packages may tumble so closely have they packed them in.
But just loading me up is an extravagance
– My thermostat setting off a hum
If my versatile door is left open too long.
I come with adjustable feet, a free scraper,
And fitting a décor-panel couldn't be much easier.
My coated metal trays boast jumbo bottle trap-doors.
I am the well-insulated stomach of their home
Packed with commodities from Safeways:
Items plucked off shelves as they amble down
Brightly lit aisles, piling up the trolley.
Buy me, eat me, drink me, take me home.
Nevertheless she'll be thrifty, go for a mince without lean
Or the carton to be had for the price of two.
Mesmerized, they stagger through a wonderland of tit-bits,
Each with a price-code which has to be wiped
Across the little window at the check-out
While they go on adding to the mountain on the belt.
The receipt is an endless scroll; but the longer it gets,
The prouder he is of his pay-cheque.
It's just edible money, after all,
Dealt with by the card placed on the rack
By the girl and given a swift rub-over
To leave the imprint of a stencil on her counterfoil.

Homewards they roll, with seafood, food from the air,
Star fruit and esoteric vegetable
Stuffed into carriers which overfill the hatch-back:
Some destined for my bin, others for my shelves
Or the tall bottle storage in my door.
Somehow they get most of it in, piling excess
In the wooden bowl above my arctic recesses:
Vulnerable surplus, prompting them to diminish
What they've got by immediately eating a lot
Betwixt tall flames atop barley-twist candlesticks.
I am the provider of the chilled pick-me-up
Which stimulates metaphysics after my door has shut.
These two appreciate my comforts:
Ice-cubes expanding like investments,
Leftovers covered by saucers,
Dinners hard as the day they were bought.
I keep the salad crisp, the meat germ-free,
The milk smelling nice for a while.
And what about the sight
Of the midnight raider bending over me,
Intimately kindled by my interior light?
Meanwhile their overdraft goes up
Thanks to an increase in the mortgage rate.
He gets requests for the representation of cheques,
And monthly waves of direct debits
Break against the limit set.
Reinforced windows brood on his frozen account.
This time he's gone and got his fingers burnt.
By the hour, their passion grows more tepid.
As for the morgue which is me,
I merely take the heat out of vacancy.
Tall as a coffin, I comment on insolvency,

Nothing but a single frozen pea
Embedded in my non-defrosting box.
There's only a scraped margarine punnet
Sitting here. If disposing of a frigidaire,
Break off any catches as a safeguard
Against children getting trapped inside it.

SPLICES

Rejected Plains Indians pretend with a horse in drag.
My uncle's was the first I went to, dressed as a page
In velvet. Fun conducting the organ from
Behind the bridal train. Kept the pews in stitches,

Though my uncle disapproved.
Blackfoot wedding guns get fired
On the day of the mudbrick lampbulb. Uncle's bride
Used relic oil that year of camera dread.

I bumped into her gourd voice-disguiser.
That was a hoot. Mother kept recalling it,
Much to my embarrassment. Seemed to lack decorum:
The Blood Indians in their bicycle-chain blue jeans.

Next was the grand union of the Mozambique pianos.
Everyone came to *their* breakfast.
We got hitched ourselves dangling from fishing-rods
Above the cottage roof. Now that was a high point.

A marionette at the registry pronounced us what we were,
While Marvin wolfed the buffet: he was my best man
– A Coney Island comic, punishing the pun,
While you swanned around with a red dress on.

Land commissioners in pith helmets met crocodiles
In straw hulas. All my relatives accepted
The hash cookies. I barged into your sister
Changing into less decorous attire. I kissed her.

Meanwhile the dog had finished off the cookies.
Later I came across her looking bemused.
Slowly all four legs slid away from each other.
Then she went to my mother's car to be sick.

A YOUNG MOTHER

She was weighed down by the one child;
Weighed down by the arms. Too old
For a piggy-back, they pull the shoulders
Out of their sockets. On the cover
Of a book women pulled at a rope.
The waiter set down a Martini.
They get set down and forgotten about
Or snatched up so that their handles rip.
She had forgotten to ring the station.
Her mother-in-law snatched up her son
Whose pants had ripped on a fence.
Either they come free or you have
To pay for them. Just then her eyelash
Came free of the lid. She was told
She would have to pay for the operation.
Bags carrying precious objects or perfume
Can be used again for the garbage.
Saint Christopher carried *his* load.
She wondered whether her body ever would
Be used again, the child weighed.

BIZARRE BAZAARS

Would she want a fetish? Every one of them
Distressed, and purchased wholesale by
The hecatomb. Their vendors too
Pluck at your sleeve, anxiously usher you
Into the darker heartland of their store.

Or latex as a second skin?
– But would she wear it in the shape it's in:
A headmask dangling from the knickers?
Otherwise there's little else
Except in lurid, harsh materials.

Knead your way through mounds of mixed chemises.
There are markets tucked in little squares
Where aged women seek the lids to teapots.
In your turn you scan the trestle
Tables, sift the polyesters.

Bottoms, tops, incongruous, or other more
Intimate thingies other people wore;
Choosing by feel; looking for what?
Your girl's thighs as if they were someone
Else's in these peaches and cerises?

Thrilling to finger, though,
Rubbing the nap on them, checking the textures.
Were you not so closely served,
You'd lift each item to your face
The way a Frenchman sniffs a fresh baguette.

AN INTERVIEW WITH THE SINN FEIN

Racks stacked with the softer glossies
Clutter the shop to be moved across
Whenever they expect the squad.
Here the dreck for raincoat use
On the domestic market comes
Invariably sealed in plastic.
Faithful only to selected beaver-shots
From steamy European threesomes,
All the best bits have been cut
To show our disapproval of the Continent.
Penetration has been duly obliterated
By a spot that's not to be peeled off
Because intrinsic with the print
Several generations back.
These cheapskate versions are craftily
Folded to display preliminaries
Never to be followed through
After you have ruptured your packet.
When I tried to check this out,
The big man who managed there
Told me he would break my arms
If I did any damage to his seal.
The helpful manager by the canal
Shows me how to unscrew the cassette,
Turn it over and remove the spool.

THE EROTIC WINDMILL

Enter the Erotic Windmill then,
    where, like a haberdashery, the porno shop
    is just another business to be run.
A windmill somewhere on the Rhine.
Inside its emporium negotiate
    shelf after shelf of super hardcore:
    Piquante, Schule Mädchen and so on.

Several languages are sandwiched in.
They all say the same thing
    – could be a method of study,
    should you be thinking of a foreign tongue.
Our mating shows are formal as the birds:
    this black swan insinuates his neck
    between a pair of crested cockatiels.

Tossed to love's lunatic fringes,
    acolytes spin through golden showers,
    Roman Candles and their own chocolate.
You find mags for dwarfs, amputees.
Cross references are very probable:
    a dwarf about her size may seem
    heaven-sent to a maiden without legs.

Love as grotesque as the Middle Ages
    pins our earwig motions to the tall
    vanes of the Erotic Windmill.

OASIS

This aching from a swollen vein
Obliges me to meditate
On what it is to own a skull
Since I can't get out of it.

It's as if a grain
Had got between the eye-ball
And its socket:
Makes the teeth grate.

So I stare it out
Like a stunned mullet:
Oxygen is wrong for me,
I'm suffocating on it.

Expansion of the brain
Strains every seam.
Won't drink, smoke
Or make love again.

Blissful to come down from it
In this Thai restaurant:
Feeble music, thin soup,
The slender whispering of silk.

BETWEEN FUNCTIONS

First he sticks his fingers down his throat,
Who in a moment must extemporize
On somebody's bath-house. His role
Is to stretch his concertina, not
To squeeze as much as Martial
Into a handful of lines. For Statius
Knows how to spout. His poems
Are articles on chi-chi villas,
Openings and events on the social
Calendar. Politically,
He is never less than correct;
Has nothing but praise for gallery
Owners, gladiators and the grandiose.
For Statius can never subtract.
How long can he spin things out?
The road of excess
Leads to the palace of Domitian.

THE LARDER SCENE

Where a scullion squats to accommodate
An up-and-coming merchant and his son
In a larder daubed with badly executed
Sketches, there is little room
For the niceties or for attention
To the cooking. Dishes blacken,
Sour armpits modify the afterglow;
The boy's asthmatic and his father at
The age when a man looks overdue.
That was a long time ago. The guide
Squeezes in some thirteen tourists
Who admire the slattern – after all,
Art is what they've come for, isn't it?
But how these voyeurs must constrict
The ghosts who made it in this den,
Paid their pence and pinched the cheek
Before the ash rained down and did them in.
Now the guide hurriedly salutes the tourists
As they step outside, leaving evidence
Of their appreciation in his palm of course,
Before they board their coaches bound
For Paestum or the Amalfi Coast.
By sunset, installed along a corridor,
Eager, now they find themselves in privacy,
For images which occupied their minds,
Whether the windows offered waves or vines,
They reach for zips, then proceed with cursory
Preliminaries to conjure up the larder scene.

In the lounge below, a single traveller
Among the party riffles magazines
Unseeingly, and punctuates her thoughts
With surreptitious glances at the bartender.

CASTEL GANDOLFO

The old table has been thrown over the balustrade
Into the crater where the fig trees choke
And dovecotes are hidden by liana.
A bland gorilla postures in a glade,
While house music billows up like smoke
Out of the sunlit mirror of Diana.

After libations, jays get on the nerves:
Wrecked at the station, willing a train to appear,
I contemplate the rails' rusted patina
Through the ebb and flow of my reserves.
A bed of stones accommodates the sleepers here:
Nuts too rusted to unbolt jiggle on the retina.

Stillness is conferred at last by those etherial
Spears of iris underneath the conifer.
Then the bowl mists over, fading out the peak,
With its head-dress of gantry and aerial:
Tight drums on high places sacred unto Jupiter
Register the signal and monitor the squeak.

Lynxes glide past the sentry-box at the gate
Guarding that invalicable zone which never thaws
Even when Domitia leads Paris through the brake
Down to the nymphaeum, and closer to his fate,
As the emperor is towed by a boat with muffled oars
Into utter stillness at the centre of the lake.

Black trees trace their shadows on the brink's
Unfathomable blue, as the popular male
Pulls out of her, and his odour grows
Rich in her nostrils, mingling with lynx
And sweet chestnut, while a vapour trail
Fades above the lairs of these extinct volcanoes.

DEATH LANE

Beside a heap of broken tile,
The worn sole of gumboot
Left to perish on the clinker
Strewn about some pyramid
Saddled with a look-out.

Whose club was this, if not
Those back from colder walls,
The wax still unvarnished on
A god's new plans for the *Limes*
Or a tunnel worthy of his aqueduct?

Whose tomb was home,
Entrenched in a court with a palm,
A big palm, then nothingness
And bricked-up entrances
Behind squared verdigris?

'Let your last bunker be
Our mutual columbarium;
A dormitory of crooners
In a dovecote for departeds
Bordered by the slim oleander.

Papyrus in the pool, pomegranates,
We assure you, somewhere,
Ilex, and every sort of laurel,
Sad green and fragrant laburnum,
And asphodel, asphodel as well.'

Munching on those pungent bulbs
Must be what's responsible
For bare-breasted girls
Lying in their lovers' laps
Under Fiat steering-wheels.

Dying in each others' arms
Between the earth's breasts
Coming up Etruscan out of cinders.
Acanthus is a blemish though
On the drab nipple of Horatius.

Out past the catacombs,
On beyond the staging-post,
Nine miles of bust chairs, mattresses.
Wild barley country now
Wedged between the motorways.

By early spring, their chariots
Will come to park and woo
Behind this mausoleum
Eaten almost through by excavation
Which revealed absolutely nothing.

Squashed couples wriggle up
Into vests, chemises,
Then tip their seats back
And rummage for another nail
To drive into the coffin.

The Old Roman

The commune couldn't give a damn,
So long as Helios goes down,
Red and smokey, over their
Funerary road for crumpet
Half a mile from the hippodrome:

Pink towers and circumstance;
Post-modernist Roman
Wisteria extends across
This august stadium
Near the old road to Brundisium.

Beware, though, of the lemur
From the last resting-place of Romulus,
Whose father gave a circuit to the dead
Because he had it in him
To appreciate the races.

2

The Ballad of the Sands

THE BALLAD OF THE SANDS

She kicks off her shoes
As the season winds down.
It's cheaper on the rides,
But when she's got the blues
She usually decides
To go barefoot on the dune.

The Pelican Hotel
Boasts a good view of it
Looming over trees
Between swung swings
And children on the rungs
Of the amenities.

Trippers crack jokes,
Filling to the brim
Bins for their crisps
While balancing their smokes
On tables where the booze
Froths along its rim.

The moron on the patio
Cannot help but stare:
He leans against his minder
Afflicted with a glare
And seems to have arms
Where his legs ought to go.

To lug him or his friends
Up the steep sands,
The keeper at the gate
Loans toboggans at weekends,
Not that they accelerate
In anything but snow.

Here the sun intensifies
The tamarisk, and toe-grips
Collapse on a haunch.
The calm profile gets
Interrupted by silhouettes:
Each step setting off an avalanche.

The dune serves as prostitute
To loud sneakers now:
Hardly any foot
Of her without scuffed print.
Dogs, balls, men;
Jeans, bleached women –

They photograph toboggans
Which refuse to budge.
A dog's bark begins
To break the frail crust
Still intact, higher up
On the last ridge.

A sky swamped moon
Rises as the dune rises
Over plantations of pines.
The marram grass
Pierces her with sparse
Tufts poking up like spines.

Stiff, bleached marram,
Every plume and stalk
Shaking as the girl
Continues her solitary walk.
The bare feet fall
Without a sound.

The girl has no goal.
Savouring her wanderlust,
She brushes through the thickets
Inhabited by crickets
Till she wades the gust
Battling her skirt.

Her footprints are soon
Smoothed over by the wind
And you lose their descent
In some crater of the dune
Where the shade's crescent
Enlarges afternoon.

Boys shout bang from the ground.
But out of sight
Is clogged of sound,
And even further away
There is the sea, glittering
In stretches blurred by grey.

Flat-bottomed, bumbling
Cumuli address the coast:
Did the children pass her
At a run – tumbling
Because the steep
Impelled them all too fast?

Lower down, the dune
Gets caressed;
Losing all marks
Of upsets and mouthfuls of sand.
The breeze is the ghost of a hand
Moving over a breast.

A gnarled tree reaches
Under the skirts of a cloud
As you roam the beaches
And every tufted pass
Calling for the blue girl
Lost among the marram grass.

Orange berries glow
As the tamarisks encroach
On the dune: a slow
Drift of ripples
Volcanic in approach,
Or lava worn as a broach.

She might pick a spray
To set off her suit
As she makes her way
Through the streets to work.
Bushes of this sort
Deck the tiered court.

She wears dark tights
And a tube skirt
Slit up the back.
Her high heels clack
Down the brick steps
By the lights.

Here the motors wait,
Easing off their brakes
And ready to accelerate
As others move across.
A sleek Rover overtakes
A double-decker bus.

Three flowered frocks
Get stranded on an island.
Someone dashes past
In a cardigan with mail
As a messenger locks
His bike to the rail.

Here the traffic
Trembles for the girl
Stepping out into it
As the lights change
And the wheels whirl
And she skips out of range.

Here the old Roman
Catches his reflection
As he glides past the bank
At the intersection
And swings round the taxi rank
In his dented Datsun.

Back in town again
After a day of triple lane,
Two direction curves,
Where the broken line
Altered sides from dip to rise
– A day full of swerves.

He drove on his own
Dazzled by the sun,
And his steering gave a groan
At each slow turn
– Groaned as in pain.
Back in town again:

A man who haunts
The venues of the young:
Lemur of his own youth,
Never mind the taunts
He may fling at himself,
On occasion staring at the truth.

Out of tune with his career,
This sham emperor
Cruises through the town
From sauna to singles bar,
Searching for some elixir
In a dented motor-car.

Pale old Roman:
He may be balding,
But he's no eagle, this one.
A hedonist at heart
With an outer shell
Which hasn't worn well.

Habitué of crowded pubs,
Connected by his eyes
To any parts in contact:
Brisk young thighs
Pushed against hips,
Reciprocating lips.

A surreptitious glance
And a half bitter smile
Establishes his stance;
A single man once more,
Answerable to no one,
What is he searching for?

The whiskey sour
In the right hotel
At the happy hour?
The attentive belle
Raised from the floor
At the end of her straw?

He is the attentive one
The lady in the navy suit
May notice drinking
At some adjacent table.
He's not that cute,
And she knows what he's thinking.

An hour later, therefore,
He seats himself gingerly
On a bench already wet
With condensation or
Some other person's sweat.
Sour steam surrounds him.

He soaks up the heat,
Tries to free his mind
Of its image of a girl
Observed on a dune
Battling the wind:
A girl like the moon.

She looked blue, beautiful.
But now his session's up.
He vacates the steam
As a blond, busty treat
In pale aertex freshens up
Each dank corner of the suite.

Here he is again,
Limper now, but clean,
Cruising through the streets
With stars in his sights
– Or are they just the lights
Reflected in his glasses?

Nice if he could score,
But he doesn't take
Enough care anyway.
The core of a pear
In his key-tray
Shouldn't be there.

Somewhere in the eighties
He lost the art of chatting up.
Getting laid is serious
For an unassuming chap
Saddled with the tastes
Of a Tiberius.

Absent-minded
When he's on the hunt,
He glides past the moon
In his Datsun saloon
With the dent at the back
And at the front.

He glides past the starred
Lugubrious hotel,
Where old turds gather
In the stair-well,
Queuing for the lecture
On the Bard.

He ought to be there,
Not heading for the disco
Along from the fair
At the far end of town,
Just up the shore
From the marram-covered dune.

The wenches go out there
In their Lycra underwear,
Soon to be upended
By the Zipper:
They shriek down chutes
And they wail on the Dipper.

The Cyclone Twist
Isn't to be missed,
But later on
They like to frisk
Around their bags
To the latest disk.

Chic teen dreams
Flicker in the beams
Of the syncopated spots
Till the fog-machine
Messes with their curls
And they join the other girls.

One of them has been
In trouble with the Law –
Not for nothin serious, mind.
Call one a whore,
But the rest are amateurs,
Partially inclined.

And though she would rather
Be sampling the rides,
The one in the turquoise
Hiccups and confides
In the eager gentleman
Who could be her father.

She spits as she chatters,
Passionate and squiffy;
Pressing where it matters
And giving him a sniffy;
Boasting that she lifted
Her perfume from Boots.

Wonderful sensation
Of spittle on his cheek
Spat from such lips,
And he likes the reek
Of tobacco on her breath
As she slags off probation.

She hasn't done time,
And she's not on the game,
And she has a feller,
But they're all the same
– Young men at least:
They get you all creased.

With an older bloke though
A girl can depend
On a drink for herself
And one for her friend:
What matters at the disco
Is what you've got to spend.

You seat her in the dark
Of your comfortable saloon,
Slap in a cassette,
Turn the volume down
And take her to the carpark
Out by the dune.

Uncertain what she'll ask,
You offer her a swig
From your flask;
And then in lieu
Of further talk
You suggest a walk.

The big full moon
Diminishes the stars,
Hones every shadow
To a knife's edge.
A tree's dead spars
Appear dim though.

What is it moves
Out of the sand
In which it has sunk?
It's only a trunk.
Utter darkness
Rustles in the groves.

The moon shines bright
Between grey fleeces:
Her radiance increases
The bowl of the dune,
Felt as very large
Even in the light.

She slows down the cloud,
Blazes on the creatures
Sunk in their gloom.
Imperiously proud,
She travels by the light
Of her features.

Having spilt love,
You're too dazed to move;
And though you should be brisk
The moon numbs your feet,
Roots you to the spot
By the tamarisk:

The place off the track
Where she said
She'd had enough
And wanted to go back;
The place where you dug
The shallow trough.

She may not follow,
But you must get away
From the hollow
Where she started to shout.
Time is the sand,
And yours is running out.

Nothing shines so brightly
As the white ball of light
Bearing down from afar.
Prints remain visible
On this illuminated night.
You must get back to the car.

Melancholy hooting
Floats across the motionless
Ripples which cover
The flanks of the dune
You stumble over.
Dawn will come soon.

Next will come the minder
Who tugs the moron
Through the sandy places
In a hired toboggan,
With little else to do
But follow up your traces.

You are completely alone
With the dune and the moon:
Sufficiently high
To catch the lighthouse
Many miles away
Flashing once, then twice.

On this saddleback of sand
Gusts and eddies move
Her grains into a collar-bone;
A long, curved ridge
With a sharp edge above
The steep plunge down.

The pine plantations sough.
You are about to go down
Into a cleavage of time
Occluded by a cloud
Fashioned like a clown
Which is changing even now.

It has become the skull
Of some tormented girl,
Her mouth open wide.
The moon disturbs her mane,
Passes through the fringes
Of her brain.

She gets lost inside,
And the world goes dark
Before you get back
Through the pines
To the carpark.
Everything looks black.

But she sails through the cloud,
And her radiance comes back;
And the whole dune glints
And shimmers as you'd wish it,
If those damn prints
Didn't somehow blemish it.

Creakings in the pine trees.
You slip past the corpses
Of wart-hogs –
Or are they logs?
You just make the Datsun
But can't find the keys.

You can't have locked them in!
Not in the ignition!
Absent bloody minded
By your own admission,
Now you're stuck, blinded
By their dangling.

For in between the blackouts
Perpetrated by the clouds,
As a chill enshrouds
The carpark in silence,
The moon grows intense
And uses these to dazzle you.

NOTES

Page

11   'Talking of Michelangelo' was written on the occasion of an Alex Katz show at the Whitney Museum in New York, but the 'helpless / Girl on a bed' alludes to a painting by Lucian Freud.
12   The 'Melancholy Isle' is Tobago. A manchineel looks very much like an ordinary, rather green apple, however it is very poisonous.
27   'Bizarre Bazaars' is set among the flea-markets of Paris.
34   'Death Lane' was inspired by the Appian Way.
37   In 'Castel Gandolfo', Paris refers not to the town but to the celebrated mime of the first century.
41   'The Ballad of the Sands' is written in a verse-form pioneered by F. T. Prince, where, in a six-line stanza, two rhymes must occur, though in any order, while two lines are at liberty not to rhyme. The form mediates admirably between strict construction and *vers libre*.

About the Author

Anthony Howell was born in 1945. After an early spell dancing with the Royal Ballet, he has concentrated on poetry and performance art. In 1973 he was invited to the International Writing Program in Iowa, and in 1974 he founded the Theatre of Mistakes, a performance company which made notable appearances at the Cambridge Poetry Festival, the Paris Biennale and the Hayward Gallery, as well as in New York. He has published five previous collections of poetry and a novel. Now a senior lecturer in Fine Art, living in Cardiff, he is editor of *Grey Suit*, a video cassette for art and literature, which is published quarterly and features poetry, performance and avant-garde film.

Books by Anthony Howell from Anvil

NOTIONS OF A MIRROR

'The best of Ashbery's English disciples is without doubt Anthony Howell, and his volume *Notions of a Mirror* deserves the attention of anyone who cares for poetry at all.'

— ROBERT NYE in *The Times*

WHY I MAY NEVER SEE THE WALLS OF CHINA

'[He offers] so much good poetry that one is astonished that Howell's name is not better known. He has a finely attuned eye and ear ... If Howell were only a descriptive writer, that would be refreshing; but he is a thinker too, and the scaffolding of reason he erects raises his poems to distinction.'

— JOHN GREENING in *Poetry Review*

'His new collection is long and intense, but at no time difficult to follow. Most of the poems celebrate travel and the uniqueness of places, and they include the best poetic account I've read of the ecstatic miseries of air travel ... Howell has style to spare and is happily unclassifiable.'

— PETER PORTER in *The Observer*

HOWELL'S LAW

'I read it ['Boxing the Cleveland'] all of four times, gluttonously, and have memorized whole chunks ... The poem surprises with its depths – but all the poems in *Howell's Law* are surprising in some way ...'

— SYLVIA KANTARIS in *Poetry Review*

'Well-made yet open-ended poems on a bewildering variety of themes ... ['Boxing the Cleveland'] is one of the most splendidly sweatily *physical* poems I have read for years.'

— ROBERT NYE in *The Times*

'In his elegance, his clarity of eye and mind, his quickness and range of reference, and his wit, Howell is a constantly rewarding read. Always entertaining and thought-provoking, he can also engage the emotions. Warmly recommended.'

— GLYN PURSGLOVE in *New Welsh Review*

New and Recent Poetry from Anvil

HEATHER BUCK
Psyche Unbound

TONY CONNOR
Metamorphic Adventures

CAROL ANN DUFFY (ed.)
Anvil New Poets 2

HARRY GUEST
Coming to Terms

MICHAEL HAMBURGER
Collected Poems 1941–1994

JAMES HARPUR
A Vision of Comets

MARIUS KOCIEJOWSKI
Doctor Honoris Causa

PETER LEVI
The Rags of Time

CHARLES MADGE
Of Love, Time and Places
SELECTED POEMS

DENNIS O'DRISCOLL
Long Story Short

PHILIP SHERRARD
In the Sign of the Rainbow
SELECTED POEMS 1940–1989

RUTH SILCOCK
A Wonderful View of the Sea

SUE STEWART
Inventing the Fishes

A catalogue of our publications is available on request